lost without Him

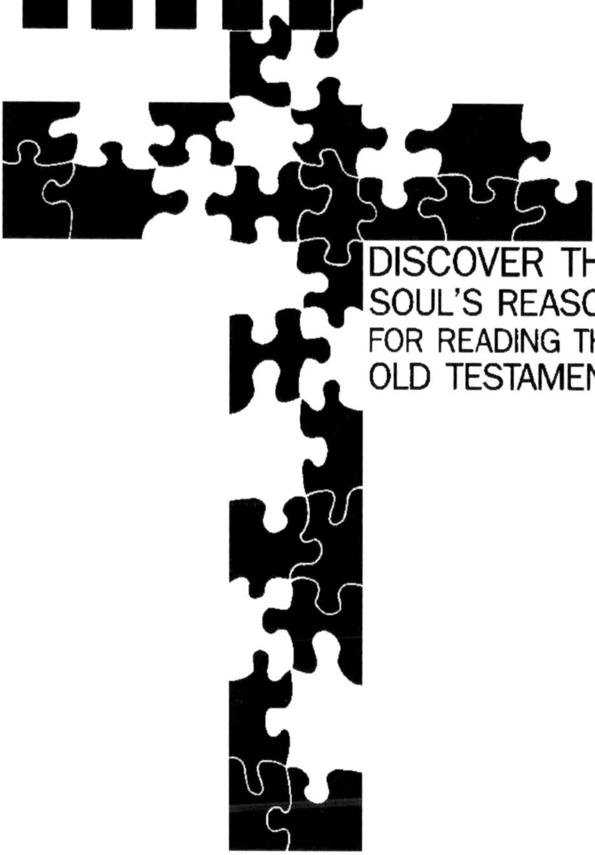

DISCOVER THE SOUL'S REASON FOR READING THE OLD TESTAMENT

Revised Edition, Third Printing January 2015

Original front and back cover art by Ben Branum
Original art (Page 21) by Minister Frank E. Frazier
Desktop Publishing services provided by Nekheti Nefer-Ra

Land, Pastor William E.
Lost Without Him:
Discover the Soul's Reason for Reading the Old Testament

ISBN 978-1-62407-766-1

St. Albans Church of God in Christ
678 Aurora Avenue
Saint Paul, Minnesota, 55104
United States of America

Reviews

"Pastor Land has written a simple and helpful introduction to a Christian reading of the Old Testament. The best way to make use of Pastor Land's work is to begin your own journey through the Scriptures."

Pastor Rich Johnson
Fairmount Ave United Methodist Church

"I firmly recommend to new beginners starting their faith walk and to believers that you add this book to your spiritual library as a reference guide...because its clarity and boldness will help you unlock the hidden secrets of the bible that will light your pathway to a new reality in Jesus Christ our Lord."

Reverend Gerald Othella Garth

"Witnessing the transformation of what started as a study guide into this book has been a treat! This little jewel will whet your appetite for a thorough reading of the Old Testament."

Denise King
St. Albans COGIC

Table of Contents

Foreword

Worship and service, in the kingdom of God, must be informed by truth – biblical truth (John 4:24). As the events of the book of Acts unfolded, people from many countries gathered in Jerusalem to worship the one true and living God. A man from Ethiopia was also there to worship (Acts 8:26-40). To grow in his knowledge of the truth of God, the man obtained a copy of the book (scroll) of Isaiah, which he read as he began his return trip home. But, like all of us, the man needed guidance to fully understand biblical revelation. So the Lord dispatched Philip, a preacher and leader in the first century church, to ensure that the man understood that Jesus Christ alone is indeed the Lamb of God who was slain for the sins of the world (John 1:29). When the man understood that the suffering Savior, Jesus, is also the Son of God, his life was transformed. He trusted in Christ for salvation, Philip baptized him, and the man *"went on his way rejoicing"* (Acts 8:39). No longer *"lost without Him,"* the man from Ethiopia was overjoyed in the salvation and newness of life that Christ alone could provide.

In every generation, the Lord provides preachers and teachers to guide us in accurately handling the word of truth (2 Tim. 2:15). Pastor William Land is that kind of preacher. His approach to ministry reminds me of the kind of shepherds that the Lord promised to send to His people – *"I will give you shepherds after My own heart, who will feed you on knowledge and understanding"*

(Jer. 3:15). This book, *Lost Without Him,* is the fruit of a shepherd's heart. The truth of God's word is the anchor of Land's faith and the foundation of his ministry. As you read this shepherd's guide of the Old Testament, your thinking will be sharpened and your faith will be strengthened. Join Pastor Land on this guided survey and you, too, will discover the *"soul's reason for reading the Old Testament."*

Terry Stephens, M.Div.
Associate Pastor
North Center Baptist Church
Brooklyn Park, MN

Author's Note

The purpose of my book is to encourage those of you who have never read or only heard about the Old Testament, to read it. *Lost Without Him* allows you to experience the Old Testament in a way that is life changing. I believe even that person who has given up reading it due to frustrations with pronouncing names, various sacrifices, seeming contradictions, etc, will desire once again to seek God through the Old Testament after reading this book. *Lost Without Him* will help inspire you to believe or strengthen your faith in God as you learn about the children of Israel. Hopefully, nothing stands out more to you than accepting the fact that choices truly matter. If you approach *Lost Without Him* sincerely, searching for the truth, chances are you won't be hesitant to read the Old Testament. Neither will you be disappointed.

To readers who are acquainted with the Old Testament, there are several fun little exercises hidden within certain statements written in *Lost Without Him* to see how well you know the stories. Although it is a simple read, it's great for study groups of all ages to learn how to connect prophecies and locate particular scripture readings, as well as to remember who says what. My objective is to challenge you to answer over one hundred questions asked in this book. These are the details the casual reader may not know. After reading *Lost Without Him*, I hope you find the urge to talk about it hard to suppress. Once you tell someone about this book, get ready to have a great discussion on the Old Testament.

Personally, putting this book together has been a very challenging test to see how much I knew about the Old Testament. If you only knew all the discussions that went on inside of my mind, trying to figure out what to and what not to mention in the Scriptures, then you would understand how rewarding this is for me to complete. Without the Holy Spirit inspiring me to write this book, I would not have put forth the effort necessary to be stretched beyond my personal abilities. *Truly, I am lost without Him.*

Introduction

Whenever you approach the Bible, it is very important that you are not drawn to particular books while neglecting others that are just as potent as the ones you may select. By committing yourself to the whole content of Scripture, there within the pages of the book is a beautiful revelation from God to all those who love and seek Him. Notice, I say *"books"* when referring to certain ones you may find more enjoyable than others. However, when I mention *"book,"* my intent is for you to focus on the fact that the entire Bible is God's revelation to us.

Although there are two Testaments, make no mistake about it – the messages harmonize into one. I hope that you prayerfully read with anticipation and allow the greatest blessing known to humankind to be revealed in your heart. This is a passionate look into the Old Testament for that person who is interested in learning about it. Not one verse, which means genealogies, prophecies, laws, ceremonial rituals, the annihilation of entire tribes, psalms, proverbs, and end-time predictions, should be viewed as unnecessary to learn. Everything is written to challenge your mind to think, hope, persevere, and trust that you'll *"understand it better by and by."*

Before I go into the Old Testament, I want you to think about a statement I heard my Pastor, Superintendent Timothy Barge, who is now at home with the LORD, say: *"The Bible is like a jigsaw puzzle. Unless you know what the picture looks like, you'll never figure out the puzzle."* Whether it is Old or New Testament, it is obvious that some of the stories in Scripture are scattered. So don't become frustrated when you discover that many of the events that happen in the Bible are not always in chronological order – neither are the books. Sometimes the rest of the story is found elsewhere. Even if the Scriptures were arranged perfectly, without the help of the Holy Spirit, the Scriptures still are impossible to explain. For Job 11:7 (NEB) states, *"Can you fathom the mystery of God; can you fathom the perfection of the Almighty?"* In other words, unless the LORD makes Himself known, it is impossible for anyone to discern how awesome He is or to comprehend the excellent way in which He exists. Neither is it possible to understand His plan.

When God wants to be known, it is by personal revelation and through His word. This means each and every person must be taught. For example, Jesus' disciples have the word of God/the Scriptures (which most refer to as the Old Testament) when they begin to go into the world and preach the Gospel. St. Luke 24:27 in the New Testament tells us how they are able to do it. Listen! *"And beginning with Moses and all the prophets, He [the Lord Jesus] explained to them [His disciples] what was said in all the Scriptures concerning himself"* [emphasis mine]. This confirms my point. Although they have the Old Testament, it is still impossible to understand the essence of the Scriptures without the Lord Jesus teaching them. My prayer as you begin to read *LOST WITHOUT HIM,* is that you sense the Spirit of The Lord teaching you to understand the Old Testament.

This book starts by addressing the first 5 books of the Old Testament that are called the ***Pentateuch*** or ***Torah***. Think of them as insight for the existence of life and instructions to guide you through it. They include the Ten Commandments, Sacrificial Laws, and Ceremonial Laws. Afterwards from Joshua to Esther are the ***History*** books. From Job to the Song of Songs (or Song of Solomon) are considered the ***Poetry*** books. By the time you finish reading the ***Prophetic*** books, Isaiah to Malachi, you have read the entire Old Testament. ***Get ready to discover the soul's reason for reading the Old Testament.***

The Pentateuch

Genesis

Exodus

Leviticus

Numbers

Deuteronomy

FAITH

Genesis is the first book in the Old Testament. Chapters 1 and 2 are intended for you to listen and think about what the author is saying. He declares: In the beginning God created the heavens, earth, and everything that exists, including man and woman, just by speaking the words. Furthermore, God said let every living thing produce its own kind. According to chapter 1 of Genesis, the whole universe is very good/wondrous to His sight. Imagine for a moment seeing space, stars, and every planet in its totality. That's what God sees, and there is not one thing about it that He doesn't like.

Without mentioning everything created, the writer credits God alone for creating whatever exists. Unless you have an idea of who *this* God is, the statement *God created* makes no sense at all, especially to that person who has never heard of Him. To expect anyone to believe in God without any proven knowledge is wrong. Therefore, the writer of Genesis is informing you that:

1) God has no beginning;
2) He speaks, and everything comes into existence according to His purpose; and
3) He is pleased with His creation.

These are three good reasons to consider belief in God if you didn't know who He is. Hopefully, you will realize there is no better explanation for things created than the existence of God before created things. Try imagining nothing at all. Would anything be, including your imagination? I suggest, whenever you think of Genesis chapter 1, to remember one thing: while it's easy to accept the fact that you and the world around you exists, it's only because God has always been.

Next, it's also important to believe that the earth at this time is untainted, pure of any evil. The first man (Adam) and the first Woman (who later is named Eve) are the only human occupants. Can you think of a way to create a better world with people in it than this? Some might say that's easy. "We would just populate the earth all at once with only the type of people we desire to have. Every one of them would be purpose driven. Therefore, crime or sin would not exist because they cannot be tempted. The result is our world would also be untainted, and it's free of stress since there's no one for them to personally worry about." Do you realize how simple that sounds? Let's look closer and analyze what supposedly is a better world.

First, in that world, not one of them is related to another. By creating them all at the same time, there is nothing to link them genetically as family. Second, without the structure of family, it is an uncaring world absent of love. Third, since they can only behave the way they are made, it is also a hopeless world void of prayer and a future. Furthermore, those who suggest that world would be better than this one are obsessed with playing games. My question to them: Why create people for amusement with no greater purpose than that of toys? There are plenty of them (toys) already here.

When God creates one man and one woman, He knows exactly what He is doing. From the moment of their existence, the possibility to have the ideal experience of life and relationship is His gift to them. Although they probably don't know it at the time, to achieve the ideal life and relationship will require all human life to be connected to them. This way there will only be one race of people, and that is the human race. Every human being will have the opportunity to learn the true meaning of love and responsibility to each other and to God. No other living being on earth can gain or lose the favor of God to the magnitude of the human race.

By allowing humankind to make choices, their greatest pain and joy will depend on how they choose and react to consequences. Remember, God's gift to humanity is the possibility to have the ideal experience of life and relationship. For now, let's focus on the fact that everything pertaining to us begins with the first man and woman. Notice what happens when the temptation to defy God's instructions comes from someone they were not aware existed, especially in the manner that he appears. Prepare to hear the history of humanity.

In chapter 2, the place where they reside on earth is an area where they have access to eat everything that grows on the trees in the garden in Eden, with the exception of one. This means there is plenty of food for them.

Interestingly, a home is never mentioned. Maybe they slept on the ground or didn't need sleep at all; only God knows. However, the main things we need to know about them are written in this chapter. We also learn that Adam is a very intelligent man, naming all the livestock, birds, and beasts of the field. His wife also is knowledgeable because she is created to be beneficial to him as they learn the true meaning of becoming one. Within a matter of time, one of the beasts of the field named by Adam, supposedly with less intelligence, will put their intellect to the test. One of them is convinced that they will know as much as God their creator.

CHOICES, PUNISHMENT AND INFLUENCES

As I continue on, there are three major events that happen in chapters 3 through 11 of Genesis. **1)** ***Both Adam and his wife sin by disobeying God when they partake from the only tree that is forbidden.*** Immediately, they recognize the devastating consequence of that choice. Unless God provides a way to redeem Adam and his wife, death will await the whole human race as an unsolvable problem. Although the life span of Adam and his wife Eve will be incredibly long before physical death comes, the harsh reality of sin becomes more disturbing for them as time goes by. Sin will reside in the heart of every human being born of a man and a woman, giving the notion that something else is better than what God says. As the population increases, the human race must try to cope with the unpredictable consequences of sin.

Imagine the shock they will feel when murder, afflictions, illnesses, addictions, and deformities gradually become a part of the human experience. These trials will affect each person differently, as they seek to understand their purpose for being. Out of their need to survive they become skilled farmers, shepherds, builders, tentmakers, herdsmen, and makers of instruments as well as tools. Others will display talents. Their skills and talents are keys to help them find their purpose for existing. As you can see, they are beginning to realize their potential to care for themselves. However, it is important to know that this knowledge comes from God, who is all-knowing. He inspires in the mind ideas to meet their needs, so they are not intimidated by their circumstances.

Now that they are becoming productive, the challenge is to love one another. This will not be easy. Due to sin, self-centeredness is becoming more of a problem. Pride, laziness, anger, vengeance, dishonesty, greed, jealousy, lust, and irresponsibility are spreading throughout every family. However, there are some who truly believe in God. One in particular is known for his walk with God. When he vanishes suddenly for his commitment to God, his family continues to warn the world for generations of their disobedience to the LORD. But their success seems minimal due to so many rejecting what the messengers of God have to say.

2) ***Hundreds of years after the deaths of Adam and Eve a great flood covers the whole earth***. This is because the human race ignores the warnings of God and becomes more sinful. So God punishes them severely. With the exception of selected species and animals, only Noah, his wife, three sons and their wives find favor with God and survive by being inside an ark.

After the flood, two very important things happen. First, an altar is built to make sacrifices to God as an expression of thanks for His mercy. By shedding the blood of animals, Noah is acknowledging that there is both forgiveness of sins and salvation with God. Second, God makes a covenant with them and every living thing, declaring that the entire earth will never be destroyed by water again. Immediately, the sky becomes radiant with many colors bending through the clouds from one side of the earth to the other. From this moment on, whenever this is seen it will be a sign, especially to the human race, that the word of the LORD stands forever. I should also mention that the life span of everyone born will be drastically less than their ancestors.

3) ***Generations later, the people go from one universal language to all of them understanding only a certain language.*** This is the LORD's doing. No longer can they speak as one, which leads them further away from Him. By making language diverse, it limits the amount of influences in their lives. Therefore, they have no other choice but to separate and associate with the ones

they understand. Isolating the people will prove to be the best way to find a positive influence. Several years later, someone hears from God.

Who's Listening?

In Genesis chapter 12, a man named Abram, whom God renames Abraham, hears the voice of God and leaves his family. This man is blessed with an inheritance his family can never give him. The LORD promises Abraham land to inherit and blessings for all nations through his seed. To fulfill these promises, a miraculous pregnancy first must occur in Abraham's wife Sarai, whom God renames Sarah. At the age of 90, she will give birth to a son. Her husband will become known as the father of those who, by faith, follow the LORD's plan. The ones who choose not to follow God's plan by faith are eternally lost without Him.

Although you may not be interested in studying genealogies in Scripture, it is very, very important when you read the Old Testament that you pay attention to Abraham's genealogy, especially as it pertains to his son Isaac, and to Isaac's son Jacob. Jacob also is known as Israel, which best describes who he is; and his descendants are called the children of Israel or Israelites. God makes an everlasting covenant with one of Jacob's offspring, but that doesn't prevent the trials they all must face. A prophecy spoken to Jacob's grandfather

Abraham, over 80 years before his death, will come to pass. The LORD said his descendants will be enslaved for 400 years. No doubt, at the present time, this seems impossible. But the Israelites, consisting of twelve tribes, *do* end up in slavery.

If you study the life of Jacob in Genesis chapters 25 to 49, valuable lessons can be learned about favoritism, deception, love, reconciliation, agony, ecstasy, and peace. He lived a very interesting life. At the age of 147, Jacob dies in the land where his descendants will become slaves. After Jacob's son Joseph, his brothers, and all that entire generation dies, the influence the children of Israel have in Egypt where they live begins to fade. Soon a king rises and plots to deal with them deceitfully. Hence, Israel will experience bondage, a hardship previously unknown to them.

Several years lapse before they realize their bondage is not just in a particular place – it is also within their souls. Until they learn the importance of faith and prayer, there is no exodus for them. Almost 400 years pass before God responds favorably to free them as a people.

In Egypt, the place of their bondage, a Hebrew baby found by the bank of the Nile in a basket will one day be known as a deliverer. He is called Moses. Many years later, he has an encounter with God on the mountain of Horeb. The LORD speaks to Moses from a flaming bush that doesn't burn, telling him that He is the God of

Abraham, Isaac, and Jacob. After Moses inquires more, the LORD reveals His name as **I AM THAT I AM**. It signifies that He is the eternal God who is complete within Himself. Although it takes faith to process this, Moses is beginning to realize that he is in the presence of the Creator of all things. After the LORD displays more of His power, He sends Moses to deliver the children of Israel out of the hands of Pharaoh, the Egyptian king. A task such as this is very overwhelming alone; however he will get help from family members and others, who hope for deliverance.

When Moses returns to Egypt, the LORD works mighty wonders through his life. Ten plagues fall upon Pharaoh and his people before he lets the children of Israel go. It takes the Passover to convince him of his limitations to protect the one he loves. During the Passover, lambs were selected, slain, and eaten. By putting the blood of the lamb on both sides and across the top of the doorframes of the home where it took place, death passed over the firstborn male. While the children of Israel celebrate this day, death affects Pharaoh and his followers. His rejection of God forces him to deal with the devastating loss of his son and the children of Israel's exit from Egypt.

Still, they are not totally free from him until God parts the Red Sea and they cross on dry land. Humiliated by the loss of his kingdom, Pharaoh and his army go after the children of Israel. Those that attempt to cross the Red Sea on dry land after them are covered by water and drown. The children of Israel give thanks to God and celebrate their freedom. It will forever be remembered as one of the greatest defeats of all time. This will be a reminder to them of how God interceded on their behalf. Soon a system is put in place for someone to intercede before God on their behalf. For now, let's see how well the children of Israel behave now that they are free.

Remember these words: a celebration is only a shallow expression of joy masking the fear of what lies ahead, while joy is the highest form of celebration in the face of that which is considered frightening. Keep in mind: although the threat of Pharaoh is behind them, they haven't reached the Promised Land yet. Notice what happens next. Only three months after leaving Egypt, while in the desert on Mount Sinai (Horeb), Moses seeks direction from the LORD away from the people. When he returns to them, the elders and the people agree to adhere to the Lord's instructions so that everyone is on one accord. So Moses again returns to the LORD briefly, this time with their commitment to obey Him.

Not long afterwards, Moses also appears before the LORD another time alone and He establishes a covenant with the children of Israel on two tablets of stone. In the meantime, the people are beginning to question the length of Moses absence. It becomes apparent that the children of Israel are infested with a bunch of instigators who still have Egypt in their hearts. Their influence over the people plants the seed of doubt in the leadership of Moses, and God who delivered them out of the hands of

Pharaoh. It isn't long before the majority of them are engaging in false worship.

God, being fully aware of their activity, admonishes Moses to return to the people. After witnessing their blatant disrespect for God, Moses is outraged. The covenant that is meant to bring them into a better relationship with the LORD is broken before it can be implemented. Subsequently, repentance will spare most of them, while the rest will receive a punishment that is fatal.

Eventually, the children of Israel receive the written law given to Moses from God that can give them a new identity as God's chosen people. They are to worship Him as the only true God, live morally amongst each other, obey dietary laws, adhere to dress codes, and respect the laws that discipline bad behavior. The LORD even sanctions a day for rest that will have eternal significance to all who believe in Him. Also included within the Law are ceremonial cleansings and rituals for justification, atonement, sanctification, and glorification.

However, these ceremonial cleansings and rituals are not sufficient enough to wash the children of Israel thoroughly because they are constantly repeating them. This is a reminder to them that the stronghold of sin is not yet eradicated from their lives. No wonder they are never satisfied and constantly complaining! Although God is meeting their needs as they travel for years through the wilderness to get to the Promised Land, sin is robbing them of joy and contentment in their souls.

That is why the LORD requires from the children of Israel animal sacrifices under certain conditions to temporarily cover their sins and his wrath against them. The sacrifice had to be a firstborn male without defects or blemish, otherwise it was not acceptable unto the LORD. Also, whoever offers the sacrifices or performs the ceremonial cleansings and rituals must be declared holy to fulfill all their duties. Even though animals and imperfect people are incapable of living holy, the LORD still requires this sacrificial system to be done. Have patience; eventually you will really appreciate these observances because hidden in them, God's plan will unfold to eternally redeem the human race, which is lost without Him.

As you follow their path closely, the Savior will come like a seed that sprouts in its season. He will handle the word with skill as only God could have. His message will soothe and convict the souls of the multitudes that follow Him. It was prophesied, even before His birth, that Someone will shed His blood and become the perfect sacrifice by fulfilling God's promise to Israel first, and to the rest of the world, for forgiveness and redemption. Like a shepherd who protects his flock, He will secure the hope of everyone who believes in Him when He solves the problem of death by overcoming it. This Person is the Savior for the entire world.

In the meantime, God's choice of Moses to lead the children of Israel out of Egypt is proof of His love for them by providing what they needed. It took a humble man like Moses who could acknowledge that his sins disqualified him to be a leader of God's people. Yet his faith embraced the mercy of God, who qualifies those who are chosen to become leaders of integrity. Under the leadership of Moses, other nations feared the children of Israel because of the favor the LORD has shown them. Before you go into the history books, it is important to know the children of Israel grieve over the death of Moses, the man many of their parents and grandparents so frequently opposed. Also, the books you have just gone over (the Pentateuch) are mostly written by him.

HISTORY BOOKS

JOSHUA
JUDGES
RUTH
I SAMUEL
II SAMUEL
I KINGS
II KINGS
I CHRONICLES
II CHRONICLES
EZRA
NEHEMIAH
ESTHER

Commitment, Challenges and Courage

After wandering in the wilderness for 40 years, only 3 who left Egypt see the land promised to their ancestors. The generations born in the wilderness also see it. Praise God for remaining faithful to His Word! As the children of Israel move forward, He will destroy the walls in their way. Under the leadership of Joshua (Moses' successor), most of the children of Israel enjoy probably the most prosperous and peaceful time of their history because God fulfills every promise He makes to them. After Joshua's death, the elders and that generation also reap the benefits of peace and prosperity for serving God. It is important that you add the knowledge you are learning from these books with that of the first five books, and believe God to tear down obstacles in your way as He enriches your life.

I encourage you to read the history books. If you read these books, list the leaders you admire, such as judges, priests, prophets, and kings. Don't be surprised; there are also some extraordinary women in the history books. By identifying with certain individuals as you read, reading becomes more interesting. Study their faith, doubts, fears, and arrogance; and learn how humiliation is the only way for one particular individual to see his need for God. Believe me, at times you'll find these books extremely difficult to stop reading because the echoes of hope are heard as the pages turn. The book of

Ruth is definitely one to read. In it is a beautiful love story that mentions a kinsman-redeemer. Learning to whom that represents in the fullest sense is very important for their salvation – and ours.

As a warning, there are places within these books when God's judgments may seem too harsh. Here are two examples. God will command leaders at times during war to order the killing of their enemies, without sparing the children. The same command is given against the children of Israel, His own people, when some of them who know better disobey orders that cause tragedy to come into the lives of others who have nothing to do with their disobedience. Perhaps this seems unjust, taking the lives of children you deem innocent; but only God can authorize the taking of lives without minimizing their relevance for being. By sanctioning their deaths, maybe God spares them from a judgment far worse, which could have been possible due to the influence of their wicked parents. Although you may not agree with His methods, for us who put our trust in Him there is consolation in knowing that the LORD has an eternal plan far better than the world we see now.

As an alternative you could choose not to believe in God at all. How then will you cope with the loss of innocent lives without becoming calloused, numb, and hopeless? Since you have denied the existence of God, the only way to get justice is through an imperfect judicial system or personal retaliation. Human justice can only release, punish or kill the perpetrators; but that does nothing for the victims whose lives are unjustly taken. Their lives are gone forever, and so are the criminals whose lives are extinguished by execution. As a matter of fact, the fate of every person who dies is obliteration. Therefore, to say one life is better than another is only an expression said to the living, because the dead surely can't hear that compliment. As you can see, denying the existence of God makes justice impossible to achieve.

At least our God, who is eternal, has a purpose for every life conceived. He knows their heart and thoughts in the fullness of their existence. And when He speaks, even the dead hear His voice. *I suggest that you pray for more understanding and faith to trust the LORD, who is Sovereign, to show eternal grace to the faithful and eternal justice to those who deserve punishment. Trust me, you'll never find better answers to the tough questions about life than the ones given in the Scriptures.*

Remember earlier I said humanity's greatest pain and joy will depend on how they choose and react to consequences. Notice how Israel is like one huge roller coaster – up one moment and down the next. They seem always to be one thought away from something destructive. Israel requests an earthly king to rule over them instead of the sovereign LORD who protects them. After several warnings, God grants their request.

Years pass and then Israel's king sees an enemy he can't conquer. Right when you think these people are doomed for destruction, God sends a small solution for their giant task. To their surprise, a shepherd boy who seems unequipped to fight the enemy will defeat him. He will become the next king of Israel. His name is David. As king, the LORD establishes a covenant with him that lasts forever. David will be called "*a man after God's own heart.*" I wonder, will you feel the same if you read about David's life in First Samuel chapter 16 to Second Samuel chapter 12? From these lessons you learn the value of faith, as well as the woes that are the results of disobedience. David's son Solomon will succeed him as king over Israel. He will be known for his wisdom, wealth, and for building the temple.

By the time the fourth king is appointed, a rivalry ensues that splits the tribes, producing two kings and kingdoms. Judah becomes the southern kingdom with one king, and Israel becomes the northern kingdom with another king. Each kingdom has its own calamities. As the kings and people change over generations, refusing to listen to God's messengers is a common practice amongst most of them. Time and time again the deception of sin convinces many of them to believe disobedience and rebellions against God's will are more rewarding than obeying Him. Soon everything considered dear to them is either taken or destroyed. There is a lot of rebuilding to do. Thank God, there are always some who still take pride in their heritage and will do whatever they can to restore that which is ruined.

By reading the Old Testament, there is so much to learn, such as what it may cost to find the true meaning of life and pleasure. In the book of Esther, her faith and the insight of her uncle Mordecai is a classic lesson as to why it is always better to deny wealth and fame than your faith. I hope your faith is becoming much stronger as you continue to learn more about the history of the children of Israel. Today a believer is blessed to have the whole inspired word of God. Before you move on to the next books, pause and thank God for those who truly know their God, as well as their history.

Poetry

Job

Psalms

Proverbs

Ecclesiastes

Song of Songs

(Also called the Song of Solomon)

Inspiration, Worship, Wisdom and Love

What does it take to inspire hope within you? I know you've heard a lot about God's people being rebellious, but many did not compromise their faith in Him. Take Job for example. You can learn from him what it really means to trust in God, even when human reasoning and feelings may suggest otherwise. Within the book of Job there are unforeseen and unimaginable trials. They appear as something evil, attempting to destroy Job's faith in God or a judgment upon him. This story could cause you to question whether you can believe in God, if you don't already. It addresses the subject of unfortunate things happening to good people. If you read it, remember this: if it's wrong to test good people with bad things, then what standard was used to determine them as being good? Keep in mind, good is the opposite of evil. Therefore, to be good you must know better, and do better. Job is proof that the best thing a human being can do is to put their faith in God.

Listen carefully as you read Psalms. It begins by describing the man as blessed who does not walk in agreement with ungodly people. Neither does he stand and take the advice of sinners to keep him on the right path. He never sits in their company listening to derogatory jokes that pertain to God or His people, which is forbidden in the law. His time is much too precious to spend hearing miserable men, whose lives are dwindling away, laughing at others to avoid the pain of seeing themselves. This man, who is blessed, finds utter enjoyment in the law of the LORD; and his life inspires hope in others that there is a better way to live. Sad but true, we all can relate to the way of the sinner. It is the common theme of life without God, where the naive are bound in hopelessness due to their inability to recognize deception and deceivers are trapped in their own deceit, thinking they are getting away.

Psalms really is a must read. No matter what your circumstances may be, there are many prayers in the book to lift your spirit. As you read, feel the agony of King David, as well as others, who cry out to God to forgive their sins. Discover how liberating it is to confess your sins as you pursue true happiness. You also will hear prayers to God to vindicate them from their enemies. Approach this book as if you are hearing it directly from them. Then you will learn how important it is to revere God, who is Holy and Sovereign, even in your solitude.

Notice how they trust the mercy of God and His righteousness as you study certain passages. Also, there are references made in Psalms to alert the children of Israel how to identify the Messiah (Savior) when He comes by statements He will make and certain things that will happen to Him. As you yearn for more of God in your life as a believer, embrace the need for patience, humility, the statutes of the LORD, songs of praise, and a place to worship. Believe me; you will need each one of them to complete your own journey here on earth. So, surrender to His plan and be taught by our omniscient God; otherwise, expect your life to be a proverb on foolishness.

To mature as a believer ask God for knowledge and understanding. The appropriate use of knowledge and understanding makes a person wise, which is the highest honor of credibility attainable to human beings. When achieved, men are known for being trustworthy and women for being virtuous. To have the ideal experience of life and relationship, understanding and wisdom must be their most treasured companions. They provide the balance needed to manage the affairs of life as it applies to working, finances, eating, drinking, even how to recognize the right man or woman for you to have a permanent relationship.

Having these attributes will help you to appreciate why truth is the foundation for love and accountability the reason for submission. Whenever *"Mr. Trustworthy"* and *"Miss Virtuous"* marry, it is understanding and wisdom that unites them together to have a happy marriage and home. When children come, their relationship with God enables them to discern the differences in the children as they are growing up. This way each child gets special nurturing to reach their highest potential in the LORD. Just think what the success rate could be for parenting if we all confronted every problem with God-given wisdom and strength!

If you're not inspired by now to get closer to God, read about the king over Israel in Jerusalem who thinks his wisdom allows him to indulge in worldly pleasures and outsmart them. From these writings you will learn that temptation does not discriminate against anyone. Neither is folly limited to a specific class of people. Therefore, never make the mistake of revering anyone because of his/her wealth or talent. Life under the sun is not about pursuing personal dreams to prove one person is better than another. The human experience is much more complicated than this. Trying to figure it out on your own is impossible to do; it's like chasing after that which you cannot catch. Eventually, the king admits that the only reasonable conclusion to draw from life is no one deserves worship but God. Govern your life by His word. Without Him there are no other sensible options left with a favorable outcome in the Day of Judgment.

The last poetry book describes the most intimate relationship written in Scripture. It is pure romance that can only be enjoyed between a man and a woman; the lover and his beloved. When you read it, notice how possessive they are of each other. Listen to the descriptive language used as they visualize each other's body and their desire to be one – body, soul, and spirit. Yet, throughout this book, before you are overtaken with that uncontrollable emotion called lust, hear the repeated warning not to awaken love until the proper time. Hidden within this dialogue is the Savior's love for His bride. I hope you enjoy every book!

Reflections and Looking Forward

Think about certain events that really caught your attention when Israel's faith appeared very questionable. Remember how during their most difficult times, the LORD's faithfulness to them is undeniable. Bear in mind how He never asks them to deny reality; instead, God reassures them that there is hope in spite of their circumstances.

Without realizing it, just by reading *Lost Without Him* you have briefly covered 22 books in the Old Testament. There are only 17 left, Isaiah to Malachi. Before you move to the Prophets, take more time and meditate on how sad it is for Israel, God's chosen people, to have suffered so many adversities during their journey to the Promised Land and onward, hoping to find the Messiah. A lot is due to their rebellion against God. This can happen to anyone who thinks they know a better direction for their life than the one God has given them from His messengers and His word. Such behavior is normal when you're lost.

Brothers and sisters, so far you have gone over the Pentateuch, history, and poetry books. Keep in mind all the events did not happen in the order written in Scripture. The book of Job may be the oldest book in the Old Testament, even though it is eighteenth in order, starting with Genesis. If you begin to read the Prophets, don't be surprised when their ministries overlap. What I mean is, some of them are prophesying at the same time. Another thing to pay attention to is at times prophecies are given as if they have already happened. It is because what has been revealed to the prophets is true to them without any more proof. This is very important to know because under the law the penalty for making false prophesies is death!

If you are really serious about increasing your understanding of the Old Testament, purchase a study bible and a bible commentary, if you don't already have them. Also, do not hesitate to use the headings in these books to research a particular subject. It is an excellent way to enhance your knowledge of the Scriptures when you need a break from daily reading. Hopefully, there are maps and charts to look at as well. This way you are able to track the children of Israel's journey and have a general idea of the dates. As you begin to learn about the books of the Prophets, know that there has always been a prophetic word for the human race from the moment of sin. Therefore, no matter where one is, God has a message for that person. ***Pray for an ear to hear what the Spirit is saying to you.***

The Prophets

Isaiah
Jeremiah
Lamentations
Ezekiel
Daniel
Hosea
Joel
Amos
Obadiah
Jonah
Micah
Nahum
Habakkuk
Zephaniah
Haggai
Zechariah
Malachi

Declaration, Rejection and Hope

The last 17 books of the Old Testament are the prophets who are assigned to declare the word of the LORD to the southern or northern kingdoms. God raises each one up for a particular time and for a particular group of people. From the prophets, God's chosen people hear frequent messages to repent and believe his ultimate plan for humanity. Other nations also hear and ignore God's constant warnings, and some of them are destroyed. Even though Israel and Judah rebel against Him as kingdoms, God remains faithful to them.

Although a prophecy is given during the reign of a certain king that none of his lineage will ever sit as king over God's people, this appears to contradict the covenant God made with his ancestors Abraham, Isaac, Jacob (Israel), Judah, and King David. Unless a miracle happens, it is impossible for both statements to be true and every prophecy fulfilled. Those who put their trust in God held on to the promises and died believing in the coming of the Messiah. Thank God for the blessing of assurance! In Isaiah, He is God our Savior. In Jeremiah, He is the LORD our Righteousness. In Daniel, He is the Ancient of Days. In Zechariah, He is the Almighty King. In Malachi, He is the Messenger of the Covenant.

Unfortunately, many still refuse to believe in the prophetic Word. You wonder; what will it take for them to believe? There are times when the Israelites are prostituting themselves, behaving like whores – and these are God's chosen people! Yet, even that isn't enough to shame many of them to repent. In one of the books, believe it or not, a prophet marries a prostitute – even though he's the messenger against immorality. Now that's a very interesting study! Then a story is told about some dry bones scattered over a valley. The LORD asks someone, "Can these bones live?" Once you realize the bones represent the children of Israel, you might think, maybe it's better to leave them dead! Also, you will read certain things that sound fictitious. Here are two examples: 1) some young men are thrown into a fiery furnace and don't get burned; and 2) a man is swallowed by a big fish and lives to tell about it. I'm not making these up! Trust me; all things are possible with God if it's according to His will. ***Have faith in Him***.

If you approach these books honestly, observe how true they are to the human experience. Sometimes there's anticipation for justice to roll like a river upon the children of Israel because of their foolish behavior. Other times pleading will occur in the soul for God to be merciful and not to consume them because of their addiction to sinning. Then there's the disappointment felt after learning that these people are perishing because of a lack of knowledge – because they reject knowledge. I must say it is very easy to be extremely critical of them, until certain behaviors seem familiar to you. That's when the personal revelation comes: ***you are just like them***.

Thank God someone was wounded for the transgressions of the whole world and bruised for all its iniquities. The LORD has placed upon Him the burden of man's transgressions. To His delight it was important that He suffer severely and die. Because there is no failure in Him, He perfectly made intercession before God on behalf of sinful humanity. Therefore, people everywhere will have the opportunity to know the true meaning of love and responsibility. To seal His promise, the LORD will pour out his Spirit on all flesh to make His spoken and written word alive in the souls of them who believe, so that this message is heard throughout the world.

Of all the literature you can read, no other book prepares you for the challenges of life better than the Old Testament. It is the soul's reason for reading it. As a believer, I truly thank God for sending the prophets who never witnessed the Savior of the world coming to earth due to their demise. However, the mission to prepare the way for the LORD was not hindered.

PROMISE KEPT

Praise God for all the children of Israel who are alive and believe in the promised seed of Abraham. They can truly say, as it is written in Scripture, *"For to us a child is born, to us a Son is given"* (Isaiah 9:6a). Do you remember this statement? *"The Bible is like a jigsaw puzzle. Unless you know what the picture looks like, you'll never figure out the puzzle."* The picture is of Jesus, the only Son of God. Rejoice! What a wonderful revelation given to us in the first chapter of St. Matthew (New Testament Book) concerning His genealogy. The miracle of salvation is realized when a virgin conceives, marries, and has a Son. He is born the Redeemer of all humankind, the Shepherd who leads humanity in the way of righteousness. Every problem known to the human experience, whether physical, emotional or mental is solvable because he is the Anointed One. Whosoever refuses to put their faith in Him is lost.

Hear the words of the Messiah in St. Luke 24:44. His statement is made after He willingly offers Himself up on the cross. Proven to be dead and buried, He rises from the dead on the third day. As the only sinless sacrifice, Jesus is able to wash away the sins of the whole world. The ceremonial cleansings and rituals, as well as the animal sacrifices once required, are no longer necessary for the children of Israel who believe in Jesus, the Christ. What used to be a temporary covering for their sins is now replaced with His righteousness that will clothe them forever. These are the words He speaks before the New Testament writings exist. He (Jesus) says unto them (His disciples), *"This is what I told you while I was still with you. Everything must be fulfilled that is written about me in the Law of Moses, the Prophets, and the Psalms."* Afterwards, He is taken up into Heaven.

Brothers and sisters, if you avoid studying the Old Testament, it is impossible to really appreciate the New Testament. By ignoring the value of the Old Testament, to declare the New Testament, is to expect people to believe it's possible to have power without a source.

I hope by reading this book you received the spark needed to pursue a personal or deeper relationship with God through the Scripture. If so; as your passion for God increases, so should your desire to reach souls who are ***LOST WITHOUT HIM.***

I LOVE YOU IN CHRIST

Biblical References

Afterword

Do you remember this statement? A celebration is only a shallow expression of joy masking the fear of what lies ahead, while joy is the highest form of celebration in the face of that which is considered frightening. By observing the children of Israel you must conclude: Many went through life pretending to have a good time with no regard for the consequences, while others found true happiness in the Lord's plan in spite of adverse conditions. This is the story of the human race. I hope you've noticed that throughout this book the devil is never mentioned. This is because the power of God is greater than all evil put together. Therefore, you are without an excuse.

Acknowledgements

Seldom do we realize the impact others have had upon our lives when they cross our path. Most times it isn't until later in life that we realize they were God sent. So many have encouraged me in my walk with the Lord; it would be impossible to name them all. I only know their labor was not in vain in the Lord. However, there are two men who really helped me more than they could ever know. They are Bob Karklin and Gerald R. Johnson, whom I met while working at Honeywell International, Inc. Their friendship and generosity will always be to me a testimony of honesty and liberality.

Also, to the ministry of St. Albans Church of God in Christ, I am limited with words to say because my heart and soul are overwhelmed with intense emotion of love and joy. Thank you!

And in memory of my most treasured friend Pastor Timothy L. Barge, Sr., who is at home with the Lord. His obedience to the call of God made wanting to serve the Lord the only choice in life. Never had I heard Christ preached the way he did!

To my Wife, Shirley, your commitment to the Lord is a testimony to so many why God ordained marriage. He knew I needed you in my life. I love you for loving me to stay true to who I am in Christ.

To Travale and Quanita, TaDarrean, Adora, William II, and Destyn, thank you for being there whenever I needed you.

To all my brothers and sisters, in-laws, my Aunt Ernestine Pruitt, cousins, friends, nieces, nephews, grandchildren Khamani and Kobe – much love to all of you from me.

Finally, this book is dedicated to two of the most influential ladies I've ever known – my mother, Elnora Land, and my godmother, Effie Clemons. Also to the best male role model I knew growing up, Uncle Booker T. Pruitt. Thank God, they have ceased from their labor in the Lord and have entered into His rest.

Special thanks to Bishop Fred Willis Washington of the Church of God in Christ, Minnesota Jurisdiction (COGIC), for the opportunity to teach a class on Old Testament Survey.

Very special thanks to Denise King who corrected my grammatical errors. Her patience and insight to truly understand the spirit in which this book was given to me from the Lord is amazing. Bless You!

About the Author

My husband, William Earl Land, Sr., is the Pastor of the St. Albans Church of God in Christ in Saint Paul, Minnesota, where he has resided since his birth. He is a dedicated man of God who loves the Lord and endeavors to reach the lost, as God has called him to do. William is a man of wisdom and integrity, and he has a genuine love for the people of God. His mission is to teach, preach, and expound on the word of God. For two years his sermons were heard on a radio program called *'Crumbs from the Master's Table Ministries,'* which he founded. From the moment William gave his life to Christ he seemed to have an intense desire to know the word of God, hoping that others would also come to understand the importance of living a life that reflects the image of Christ. His life is an example to me, our children and all who have come in contact with him.

As a young man, William was told that he would one day become a leader and an example to many. He has always been a man of true convictions and true to his faith. His mother Elnora Land's life exemplified how one should live, as well as many others in his life. William's dedication to God has challenged him to write *Lost Without Him* to encourage, and awaken others to explore God's amazing word through the Old Testament.

Shirley B. Land

Appendix

Study Questions in *Lost Without Him.* Please make sure you back up your answers with Scripture, unless the question calls for an opinion.

THE PENTATEUCH

Faith

1. Who is the writer of Genesis?

2. Who do you think Adam and his wife probably were not aware existed?

3. What tree was forbidden?

4. What beast of the field put their intellect to the test?

5. Who yielded to the temptation first?

Choices, Punishment and Influences

1. What was the devastating consequence of their choice?

2. What promise did God make to redeem them?

3. What is the harsh reality of sin that would affect Adam and his wife?

4. When did Adam give his wife the name Eve?

5. What was the unpredictable consequence of sin?

6. How old was Adam when he died?

7. Name the first instrument mentioned in the bible.

8. Who suddenly vanished?

9. After he vanished his son lived to be the oldest man in the world. How many years did the father and son live combine?

10. Name Noah's three sons.

11. What is the covenant called that God made with Noah after the flood?

Who's Listening

1. How old were Abraham and Sarah when Isaac was born? Give Scriptures to prove it.

2. With which one of Jacob's children did God make an everlasting covenant?

3. Where in Scripture did God tell Abraham his descendants will be enslaved 400 years?

4. Can you tell by order of events what each word represents concerning Jacob's life?

    a) Favoritism
    b) Deception
    c) Love
    d) Reconciliation
    e) Agony
    f) Ecstasy
    g) Peace

5. Which one of Jacob's children was known for his influence in Egypt? Give Scripture to prove it.

6. Why did Moses leave Egypt?

7. Name the two things God did in Moses' presence to demonstrate His power before sending him back to Egypt.

8. Who helped Moses?

9. Name the first nine plagues that led to the children of Israel's exit from Egypt.

10. What system is put in place for someone to intercede before God on behalf of the children of Israel?

11. What do most call the covenant on two tablets of stone?

12. Name the object of their false worship.

13. What did Moses ask them before they were judged?

14. What day did God sanction for rest?

15. How did God meet their needs?

16. Why did I say the Pentateuch is mostly written by Moses, instead of all of it written by him?

17. How old was Moses when he died?

HISTORY BOOKS

Commitment, Challenges and Courage

1. What three who left Egypt see the Promised Land?

2. Name the wall in their way.

3. Where does it say God fulfilled the promises He made to the children of Israel?

4. How old was Joshua when he died

5. Name a judge, priest, prophet, and king in the History books.

    a) A judge –
    b) A priest –
    c) A prophet –
    d) A king –

6. Now list something positive or negative about each one of them that for you was a teachable moment.

7. Name the person who was humiliated before he could truly see his need for God.

8. Who was the kinsman-redeemer for Ruth?

9. Give an example in Scripture where God's people, during war, killed everyone, including children.

10. Give an example where God punished His own people severely.

11. Who was the first king of Israel?

12. Who was the enemy he couldn't conquer?

13. Why did David believe he could defeat the children of Israel's enemy?

14. What covenant did God establish with King David that will last forever?

15. What sin did King David commit that caused the sword to never depart from his house?

16. Which son of David set himself up as king right before Solomon?

17. Name the two men involved when the kingdom split.

18. Which one was over the Northern Kingdom?

19. Which one was over the Southern Kingdom?

20. What structure got destroyed that was vital to the children of Israel's worship?

21. Name someone who was responsible for the destruction, besides the children of Israel.

22. Name a prophet who participated in rebuilding Israel's temple or the walls surrounding the city of Jerusalem.

23. Who was Esther's husband?

24. What message did her uncle Mordecai want her to tell her husband?

25. Who did this information hurt the most?

POETRY BOOKS

Inspiration, Worship, Wisdom and Love

1. In the book of Job, name two of the trials he faced.

2. Why would some find it difficult to put their faith in God, based on the story of Job?

3. Who thought these trials were a judgment upon Job?

4. How do you know Job is proof that the best thing a human being can do is put their faith in God?

5. Name a favorite prayer of yours in Psalms.

6. Now write as much as you can from memory your favorite Psalms. You must use more than 25 words.

7. Name at least two statements in the Psalms that will be quoted by the Messiah when he comes.

8. Name a proverb, or find a verse in Proverbs that mentions foolishness.

9. Name one verse that mentions knowledge and understanding in the same verse in Proverbs.

10. Find a verse for each one in Proverbs – working, finances, eating, and drinking.

11. What verses in Proverbs best describe Mr. Trustworthy and Mrs. Virtuous?

12. Who was the king over Jerusalem that most believe thought his wisdom would allow him to indulge in worldly pleasure and outsmart them?

13. What did he say is impossible to catch?

14. What did the king learn to prove that temptation does not discriminate? Select a verse in Ecclesiastes.

15. On page 35 there is a reference to the King over Israel. Read the last three sentences in that paragraph and list the two verses in Ecclesiastes they best explain.

16. In the Song of Songs (Song of Solomon) it says, "Do not arouse or awaken love until it so desires," or "that ye stir not up, nor awake my love, till he please." Explain.

17. What compliment do you like most that each one said about the other?

PROPHECY BOOKS

Declaration, Rejection and Hope

1. Who gave the prophecy that none of a certain king's lineage will ever sit as king over God's people?

2. Who wrote the prophecy on the scroll?

3. Name the king whose lineage it would affect.

4. Name one prophet that accused the children of Israel of prostituting themselves.

5. What prophet marries a prostitute?

6. Who did the LORD ask, “Can these bones live?”

7. Name the three young men in the fiery furnace.

8. Who lived after being swallowed by a big fish?

9. Who said, “Let justice roll on like a river?”

10. Where can you find, “Because of the LORD’s love/mercy, we are not consumed?”

11. Where is the scripture that says, “My people are destroyed from lack of knowledge, because you have rejected knowledge?”

12. In what book, chapter, and verse can you find these statements?

    a) Pierced/wounded for our transgressions and crushed/bruised for our iniquities.
    b) It was the LORD’s will to crush/bruise Him.
    c) He made intercession for the transgressors.

13. Where is the prophecy, "I will pour out my Spirit on all people/flesh?"

14. Although many prophets died, where is the prophecy to prepare the way for the LORD, and who fulfilled it?

Promise Kept

1. What is the virgin's name?

2. Who did she marry?

3. What was the other name for the Redeemer of mankind?

4. What prophecy said the LORD anointed Him to fix any problem?

5. Explain how what appeared to be a contradiction between the kings from the same lineage got fulfilled. Remember a certain king was told none from his lineage will ever sit as king over God's people, yet God had promised that same king's predecessor an everlasting kingdom.

Written by: Pastor William Land